THEY DIED TOO YOUNG

RIVER PHOENIX

Penny Stempel

CHELSEA HOUSE PUBLISHERS
Philadelphia

First published in traditional hardback edition
©2000 by Chelsea House Publishers.

Printed in Malaysia.
First Printing
1 3 5 7 9 8 6 4 2

Copyright © Parragon Book Service Ltd 1995
Unit 13–17, Avonbridge Trading Estate, Atlantic Road
Avonmouth, Bristol, England BS11 9QD

Photographs courtesy of Rex Features

Library of Congress Cataloging-in-Publication Data
Stempel, Penny.
    River Phoenix / Penny Stempel.
          cm. — (They died too young)
    Summary: Examines the life, career, and death of the actor
who began performing very young and succumbed to a drug
overdose at the age of twenty-three.
    ISBN 0-7910-5229-X (hc)
    1. Phoenix, River Juvenile literature.   2. Motion picture
actors and actresses—United States—Biography—Juvenile
literature.
[1. Phoenix, River.   2. Actors and actresses.]
I. Title.   II. Series.
PN2287.P48S74   1999
791.43'028092—dc21
[B]   99-12877
                                                            CIP

CONTENTS

Farewell messages for River Phoenix

It is just after 1:00 A.M. on October 31, the morning of Halloween. The stage door of the Viper Room, the latest haunt of the Hollywood young and beautiful, is thrown open. A young man with short black hair, Converse sneakers, and jeans is carried out by two young women and a man. Out cold, he looks in a bad way. But this is Sunset Strip, and early morning revelers have seen it all before. They pass on by. They don't yet know what is soon to be splashed across front pages and broadcast on every channel: River Phoenix, 23-year-old star, loved by the camera, the environmentalists, and teenage girls worldwide, is dying, right there on the sidewalk.

The Viper lies on the corner of Larrabee Street and Sunset Strip. Co-owned by Johnny Depp—star of *Edward Scissorhands*—and old rocker Chuck Weiss, it lies a stone's throw from the Whisky, the Roxy, and Tatou. Freelance photographer Ron Davis, snapper of the rich and famous, was there that night. And what he saw was seared into his memory, to play again and again. River Phoenix, the serious and clean-living star, was carried out of the club by film actress Samantha Mathis, who was River's girlfriend, and by Joaquin (a.k.a. Leaf) Phoenix, River's younger brother. There was another woman with them, Rainbow Phoenix, River's 20-year-old sister. River looked drunk; he was liquid in their arms. He flopped to the ground, and then the seizures started, first one, then another. His eyes were rolled back in his head, his arms were flailing, flying up and down. Rainbow lay on top of River, trying to suppress the movement. After the fifth seizure he went still. Later, all America was to hear his brother's anguished 911 call played over and over on radio and TV: "My brother's having seizures. I'm thinking he had Valium or something. You must get here, please, because he's dying."

4

Five minutes later, when the four-strong paramedic team arrived, Phoenix had "no pulse and was not breathing." They gave basic life support and then lifted him into an ambulance. At 1:51 A.M, after 20 minutes in the emergency room of the Cedars-Sinai Medical Center a few blocks south, River Phoenix was officially declared dead. But those who saw him on the Sunset Strip pavement have no real doubt that he died there, on a warm October night, under the curved black awning that protects departing Viper customers from the rain that never falls. River Phoenix joined the pantheon of Hollywood stars whose image retains a special luster because they never lived to grow old—James Dean, John Belushi, Marilyn Monroe—but he joined early. Phoenix lived two years less than James Dean, three less than Jean Harlow, 11 less than John Belushi.

The autopsy confirmed that there was Valium in River's system, and marijuana, and ephedrine. But it was massive doses of heroin and cocaine that killed him, doses that, according to the coroner's office, would each have been lethal on their own.

There were no needle marks, and no one knew where the drugs had been taken. Nor was anyone sure just when they were taken (drugs are metabolized at different rates by different people). But a routine police search of Phoenix's suite at the Nikko Hotel in West Hollywood after his death turned up Valium, heroin, and cocaine.

Memories of River Phoenix left outside the Viper Room

Stunned Hollywood pundits asked how this could have happened to someone like River Phoenix, a sweet-faced golden boy whose passionate concerns were saving rain forests and insuring the humane treatment of animals. What was it that went so wrong for River?

Caracas, Venezula

NATURE'S CHILD

The story begins in 1968, two years before the young star-to-be was born. A 22-year-old Jewish woman, Arlyn Dunetz, left her husband and job in Manhattan to take her chances in California. Hitching one day on Santa Monica Boulevard, Los Angeles, with a friend, the pair were picked up by a man called John. John was born in Fontana, California. He was a year younger than Arlyn, had also been married before, and had a daughter named Trust. Two days later they met up again and talked until early morning. They decided they should travel together.

They took to the road, finding work as they could. In the summer of 1970 they were earning a living picking apples on a commune in Madras, Oregon, and it was there, on August 23, that Arlyn gave birth to their first child, River Jude. River's name was inspired by the River of Life in Hermann Hesse's novel *Siddhartha*. The child of mixed destiny was born in a log cabin to a roar of approval from friends invited by Arlyn to share in the experience.

John and Arlyn, with their young child, traveled through the West searching for meaning. In Pikes Peak, Colorado, they found their purpose. Joining the religious cult the Children of God, they became missionaries, first in Crockett, Texas, where their daughter Rain Joan of Arc was born in

1973, then further afield—in Mexico and Puerto Rico, where Arlyn gave birth to Joaquin. (Rain later changed her name to Rainbow, while Joaquin also used the name Leaf.) In Caracas, Venezuela, Libertad Mariposa, or Liberty Butterfly, was born. By now John was "Archbishop of Venezuela and the Caribbean" for the Children of God.

But after two years' selfless work for the cult in South and Central America, John and Arlyn were rudely awakened from their dream. Magazines blew the Children of God apart. Leader David Berg, they revealed, was a fraud who recruited through sex. This was not the sanctuary from the hypocrisy and venality of mainstream America that they had sought, and John and Arlyn split from the sect.

John, Arlyn, River, Rain, Leaf, and Liberty made ends meet as best they could, living in a beach hut in Venezuela and waiting for guidance from a "Universal Being." And it was now that the seeds were sown for River's future. River, age five, and Rain, age three, sang hymns and played religious songs on the streets of Caracas, in front of hotels, or at the airport to bring in money for the family. Much later, River was to tell the press, "It was a great stepping stone. I learned to play a guitar there—my sister Rain and I got interested in performing. It was a neat time growing up in Venezuela in the late seventies."

It was not until 1977 that the unorthodox family unit made their way back to the U.S. Inspired by a meeting with a doctor and ex-rock star, they stowed away on an old freighter that carried Tonka toys. The crew discovered them halfway there—four kids and a pregnant mother—threw a big party for them, and gave them a load of toys. They settled in Florida. John worked as a gardener, and their youngest child, Summer Joy, was born. To celebrate their new beginning, the clan took the name Phoenix. Their previous name became such a closely guarded secret that media attention has failed to uncover it.

River Phoenix (right) in Rob Reiner's Stand by Me

FORTUNE SEEKERS

In 1978, when Summer Joy was just three months old, John Phoenix injured his back. He could no longer work, and there was no money. The family needed a new way to earn a living, and the children were eager to do their part. River and Rain, now nine and seven, began to perform in local talent contests, and River walked away with prize after prize. Arlyn became gripped by the conviction that her children could captivate the world. She mailed her old school pal Penny

Marshall, star of the TV comedy series *Laverne and Shirley,* clippings about her talented offspring, and the response—a standard reply from the head of talent at Paramount—proved sufficient encouragement for the family to begin a new migration.

In a shaky old car, the family took to the road and headed off to California to seek their show business fortune. John Phoenix was later to recall, "I said to myself: What a crazy person you are. But the stars were so bright. I just felt it had to be right."

While River's father, John, preferred privacy, Arlyn was to be the driving force in her eldest son's career. Once in Hollywood, she got herself a job at NBC TV as a secretary to the head of talent. In one move she secured herself both a crash-course in the entertainment business and an income. She stayed long enough to learn the ropes and then quit to push River. Step one was to secure agent Iris Burton to act for River and his four siblings. Burton had Phoenix on her books for most of his career, starting at age nine. "He was the most beautiful child you've ever seen, like a little Elvis," she said.

Her first move was to put him forward for TV commercials. River was picked to promote Ocean Spray, Saks, and Mitsubishi. But River always stressed that his parents sought and respected their children's views. When at age 10 the young performer wanted to quit advertising work ("I felt," he said, "that the constant lying, the smiling on cue and the product naming was going to drive me crazy"), his developing career was redirected, and Phoenix hit the L.A. TV audition circuit.

The earnest and beguiling young actor continued his charmed progress. He played guitar on the daytime series *Fantasy,* he did audience warm-ups for the show *Real Kids,* and he played cheeky 12-year-old Guthrie McFadden in 22 episodes of CBS's 1982 cattle saga *Seven Brides for Seven Brothers.* The jobs came thick and fast: in 1984 there was the NBC miniseries *Celebrity,* an after-school educational special, *Backwards: The Riddle of Dyslexia*, and an NBC pilot, *It's Your Move;* 1985 saw 15-year-old River as Robert Kennedy Jr. in *Robert Kennedy and His Times*, a guest star in Michael J. Fox's long-running series *Family Ties*, and in a lead part in ABC's *Surviving: A Family in Crisis*.

The boy Phoenix had conquered TV, but River was born to run, and his next move was to the big screen. "Some people find security in routine, but I could never live that way," he said, and the dice were still loaded in his favor. His first movie, in 1985, was a science fiction adventure called *Explorers*. Picked from 4,000 boys nationwide, River played Wolfgang Muller, a bespectacled boy genius who conjures up a spaceship in his lab and makes his friend's dream come true. By the time River was 15, he had been professionally cute for more than five years. He was probably his family's chief breadwinner. He had never been to school.

If *Explorers* established Phoenix as a serious contender in Tinseltown, his next role, won in the same year, was one of three in his career—*Stand By Me, Running on Empty,* and *My Own Private Idaho*—that touched closest to his own experiences and won him unstinting critical acclaim. For Rob Reiner's rite-of-passage movie *Stand By Me,* Phoenix was selected from over 300 would-be stars to play 13-year-old Chris Chambers, the boy from the wrong side of the tracks.

Stand By Me, based on a Stephen King novella, chronicles one summer weekend in 1958 in the lives of four boys reaching adolescence. When the fat boy of the foursome overhears talk of a dead kid's body lying next to a railway track, the friends make a pact to find the corpse, and the intimacy of the trail with its gruesome goal leads the boys to bare their fears and vulnerabilities to each other.

Like Phoenix's later directors, Reiner was a filmmaker who searched for honesty, insisting on one week of improvisation before any work started on the script, with the result that the on-screen rapport between the four boys was real. River, in particular, came up with the goods, and Reiner commented,

"You just turned the camera on and he told the truth." As a tough kid, hardened by his father's beatings, dragging manfully on his cigarettes, Phoenix gave a performance of tenderness, honesty, and older-than-his-years wisdom as he offered guidance to his young friends and faced an older gang of thugs (led by Kiefer Sutherland as Ace) with courage. "If I was your father," Chris Chambers tells tearful buddy Gordy, rejected by his father in favor of his recently deceased older brother, "things would be different." Phoenix—in real life the oldest sibling in difficult circumstances—was always to be at his best on screen when giving solace or voicing his own pain. It was this fragile sensitivity that made Phoenix ultimately unfit to withstand the multi-layered hypocrisies of Hollywood life. With typical humility, River said of this role: "In *Stand By Me* I realized that what I was creating was going to live on far longer than anything of me as a person. The characters are more powerful than the person that creates them." Little did he know how prophetic his words would be.

River Phoenix was determined that Hollywood wouldn't change him

A HEALTHY ATTITUDE TOWARD HOLLYWOOD

When *Stand By Me,* a quirky low-budget production initially given limited distribution, became a surprise hit and beat the Tom Cruise vehicle *Top Gun* to the number one slot, River

Phoenix became a Hollywood name. He knew the dangers, but at 15 he had all the confidence of adolescence that he could withstand them. "People say, the movie's so good, you're going to be the next this or the next that. Take it the wrong way and you can get really high on yourself," said the young actor, unwittingly describing his own future. "You get pampered, you hang out at a ritzy hotel, get room service at the snap of your fingers, or have a limo, which is really weird. You can change and it's sad."

But for now, the sun was still shining, and Phoenix's next movie gave him a lead role alongside a major star, Harrison Ford. It also brought inevitable comparisons with the boy-actor's own family history. In *The Mosquito Coast* (1986), directed by Australian Peter Weir (*Picnic at Hanging Rock, Witness*), Phoenix played elder son Charlie to Harrison Ford's mad inventor father, Allie Fox—the man whose mission to the Mosquito Coast turns him into a dictator who comes close to destroying his wife and family. Phoenix's Charlie was the film's narrator, and his relationship with his father became the focus of the film as the boy comes to realize that his father's genius is flawed. Weir had cast Phoenix because of the similarity between Charlie and River's vagabond, faith-led childhoods, and once again Phoenix played a wise child pitched against adversity, required to shore up his father's fragile ego as well as carrying the burden of his siblings and his mother.

When he saw the daily rushes, Weir knew that he had made the right choice. "When a big close-up would come on the screen, it was like you were a kid and you went to a film and couldn't keep your eyes off a character. It's something apart from the acting ability. Laurence Olivier never had what River had," he said.

Weir also made the right choice in casting charismatic young Martha Plimpton, daughter of actors Keith Carradine and Shelley Plimpton, as Emily, daughter of the Reverend Spellgood, a missionary. On the set, in the heat and intensity of 16 weeks location filming in the tiny country of Belize,

River with actress and girlfriend Martha Plimpton

Phoenix and Plimpton fell in love, and so began what was to be River's longest-lasting relationship.

But just as Weir observed the start of new relationships with Phoenix's peers and costars, the director also detected tensions with the young man's family—small splits now that would later lead to an increasingly complex, multifaceted persona. John Phoenix was in Belize with his son as his legally required chaperone, and Weir sensed that some of the tensions between Ford and Phoenix in the film echoed those of River and his father. "With a young person who suddenly becomes the key breadwinner of a family," Weir explained, "there's an incredible amount of rearranging of things in the family hierarchy and sometimes a tension develops, particularly with the father."

The first seeds of a double life and rebellion were being sown. While River was officially following a strict vegetarian diet, when his father was not around, according to Weir, "He'd stuff himself with a Mars bar and a Coke. It seemed a healthy steam valve." Later in his life he would turn to stronger stuff.

The Mosquito Coast was not a success—Harrison Ford's Allie Fox was simply too unappealing—and the year following its release was a low point for Phoenix. Driven by a need to move from wise child to adult star, Phoenix made two false moves. First came *A Night in the Life of Jimmy Reardon*, by writer-director William Richert (later to star with Phoenix in *My Own Private Idaho*). Phoenix took the lead role as Jimmy, a 17-year-old Casanova-with-problems living in 1962 Chicago. The film is an unexceptional tale of abortion, lost love, and entanglements with older women. Phoenix took the role even though his father disapproved of his character's promiscuity, and the only apparent gains from this dubious career-move were that River established himself both as a teen idol who could play sex scenes on-screen and as a musical talent—he wrote the theme song himself.

They Died Too Young

But Phoenix, already the responsible star most teenage girls were choosing for their bedroom wall, was unhappy about the role model he was providing. By now he had a reputation as a caring, thinking, environmentally concerned young man. "A lot of people entrust themselves to you and look up to you," Phoenix explained. "I'm speaking about a lot of teenage girls who may see the movie. I'm the monogamous type and I believe romance is more important than sex, and *A Night in the Life of Jimmy Reardon* doesn't always present it that way." He also doubted he was macho enough for the part. "It should have starred someone a bit more masculine, like Tom Cruise," he said.

Phoenix's second misguided move of 1987 was in Richard Benjamin's forgettable spy thriller *Little Nikita*. Billed second after Sidney Poitier, River played Jeffrey Nicholas Grant—an all-American kid about to join the air force academy. He learns that his parents are Russian agents. Sidney Poitier played FBI agent Roy Parmenter, the man who breaks the news to Jeff Grant that not only are his parents spies, but also rogue Russian agent "Scuba" is running amok on a murder spree with a list of fellow spies in his hands. Phoenix never stood a chance—with lines such as "I don't know what myself is," a laughable plot, and some very poor teen-romance scenes, it was a performance best forgotten. Add to this Phoenix's doubts about the negative portrayal of the Russians, and the only positive thing to be gained from this movie was the experience of working with and learning from Poitier. "He's a wonderful person and a really bright man who gave me tips about life, too, not just acting," said the earnest adolescent.

"Let's say I took those jobs out of an insecurity, out of feeling that I might never work again," said Phoenix. But together, *A Night in the Life of Jimmy Reardon* and *Little Nikita* confirmed River Phoenix as more than a teen idol worthy of cover stories on teen magazines around the world. He was also the environmentalist lobby's official pin-up. For River, fame was worth something if he could use it to promote the causes he believed in: the conservation of rain forests, ethical treatment of animals, and care for underprivileged children.

"One thing I would like to do when I have the money is buy thousands of acres in the Brazilian rain forest and make a national park, so no one can bulldoze it to put a McDonalds there," he told quote-hungry interviewers. "It's a human tragedy of immense proportions. Many native Indians are losing their homes daily, and it's going to affect both you and me, because that's where most of the world's oxygen comes from."

On behalf of the animal kingdom he expressed these views: "One of the beliefs is about harmlessness to animals. I don't believe in eating meat or using any animal by-products or contributing to suppressing animals."

Despite his fame, he wanted no more than the simple life for himself. "I want kids, a family of my own. I'd like to give them the first eight years of life in the country," he would say.

The image of an environmentally concerned young man suited the publicity machine just fine. Here was a young actor not only possessed of a face to drool over but also prepared to expound, at any given time, everything the truth-seeking youth of the '90s wanted to hear. No wonder teenage girls declared him to be the star they would most like to have as their boyfriend, while Britain's *Cosmopolitan,* pitched at an older age-group, elected him "The intelligent woman's hope of what the new generation of men will be like in the 21st century—a combination of strength and sensitivity."

As Harrison Ford's son in the 1986 film, The Mosquito Coast

*In his Oscar-nominated Best Supporting Actor role
from* Running on Empty

FAME

The spotlights were now switched full strength on the young actor, and they weren't always in his control. Of one photo shoot, he complained: "I was dressed up like a model, told to pose in certain ways, to tilt my head, push my lips out, suck in my cheeks. And I'd be so tired at the end of the day, so I'd give the damned photographer what he wanted. It was the most mortifying experience." The young boy full of faith was beginning, ever so slightly, to lose his grip.

The next project, though, Sidney Lumet's *Running on Empty*, was the movie that brought River Phoenix back closer to home and confirmed him as a serious heartthrob and an actor to be reckoned with. It won him, at the age of 17, an Oscar nomination for Best Supporting Actor. With Lumet, Phoenix was once again working for a serious director who aimed for docudrama reality, and while the camera was able to fall in love with his cheekbones and turned-up nose, River was able to play to his strengths as the son of political parents on the run—the urchin with all the knowledge, sadness, and wisdom of the street. Phoenix played Danny Pope, eldest son of post-'60s political radicals Arthur (Judd Hirsch) and Annie (Christine Lahti), who bombed a government-funded napalm factory in their college days, unintentionally wounded a janitor, and found themselves on the FBI's Ten Most Wanted List. That was when Danny was two. As the film opens, Danny is 17, and they've been on the run ever since. All he's ever known is a life of changed names, forged documents, and different-colored hair dyes. There's one more move for the family unit, and then things change. Danny is a gifted musician (a fact which allowed Phoenix to demonstrate his own prowess on the piano), and his music teacher gets him a coveted place at Julliard. Added to that, Danny has fallen in love with Lorna Phillips, the music teacher's daughter played by Martha Plimpton—still his steady girlfriend. In a pivotal scene the aspiring Romeo climbs the tree outside Lorna's window one night and persuades her to join him in the garden, where, for the first time, he confesses to someone outside his family the truth about his parents. It's the first time he's allowed anyone so close, and he'd like to keep it that way. The scene where Danny cries as he tells Lorna good-bye is one of Phoenix's most moving.

As always for River Phoenix, he played the good son and comforter, the boy whose parents lean on him in troubled times, the older son who helps make things all right for his kid brother Harry (Jonas Abry). And for *Running on Empty,* River and his role were still in harmony. On this set, the backstage rumors revealed a serious young man in touch with his past, grounded by the presence of girlfriend Plimpton and eager to learn. Costar Christine Lahti was later to report: "I drank a Diet Coke once, and he was furious with me. He was so adamant about clean, pure living."

And screenwriter Naomi Foner noted both his lack of formal education and his hunger to make up for lost time. "He was totally, totally without education," she said. "I mean, he could read and write, and he had an appetite for it, but he had no deep roots into any kind of history or literature." She bought him a collection of literary novels for his 18th birthday.

His performance as the musically gifted Danny was a tour de force. Sidney Lumet gave the young man high praise: "He's never studied formally but, boy, does he know how to reach inside himself." Asked to predict Phoenix's future hopes, Lumet continued: "I don't know what combination of things makes a star. You have to have a very strong, clear persona and you have to be a very good actor. He is both, plus he is visually beautiful. So I would say, all things being equal, he ought to have a brilliant career."

If River was later to dabble in drugs, the habit certainly hadn't started yet. Lumet took a very hard line on drugs. "When I speak to a young actor," he stated, "I just tell him or her at the start of the picture that if anything goes on I'll fire him on the spot. I'll reshoot the entire film if I have to. Aside from moral detestation, when actors are acting under the influence of drugs, the performance may be going on in their heads, but it isn't happening on screen."

And at this stage in River's career, the Phoenix family was still keeping a tight rein on their eldest son's choices of role. In publicity interviews for the film, Arlyn Phoenix talked in strict terms about Hollywood kids and drugs. "What goes on with these kids is pathetic. Look at Drew Barrymore . . . I saw it when she was nine years old. You can see how kids make show business more important than life. It's not life, it's only a job, it's only Hollywood. Then drugs come along and they change so fast you can't get a hold of yourself. Everybody knows." And in words which were to prove sadly prophetic, she continued: "Sometimes you get a script with some of these names attached to it. I don't even read it. I don't want to hang around that person for two months. I don't want to judge them. Something inside me says something went wrong for them somewhere in order for that to happen and, but for the grace of God, it might be River."

The warning signs for this vulnerable young man, whose naïveté and other-wordliness made him both desired by and ill-equipped for Hollywood, were there for those who looked. Sidney Lumet commented: "He's incorruptible in his acting. He doesn't know how to do anything falsely. If something isn't true inside him, he just doesn't know how to do it. That can be a blessing, but it can also be a curse." Screenwriter Naomi Foner, too, was aware of the echoes that *Running on Empty* had for River and his family at that point in his career. Foner believed Arlyn Phoenix was all too aware of the relevance of the final scenes of the movie to her own relationship with River. "She knew that one day she would have to say goodbye to him," explained Foner. "I think she was saying he was ready to move on."

Running on Empty garnered not only the Best Supporting Actor nomination for Phoenix, but also the Los Angeles Film Critics Award for Christine Lahti as Best Actress. Phoenix attended the 61st Oscar ceremony on March 29, 1989, dressed in a tuxedo, with Martha Plimpton on his arm and his mother in attendance. Phoenix lost to his future costar Kevin Kline's memorable performance in *A Fish Called Wanda*, but his nomination at such a young age made him an even hotter property in Tinseltown. River took it with his customary humility. "If I have some celebrity," he declared, "I hope I can use it to make a difference. The true social reward is that I can speak my mind and share my thoughts about the environment and civilization itself."

Phoenix could now afford time out to enjoy himself, so his next bit-part brought a complete change of mood as well as a role cannily pitched to a more mainstream audience. "I wanted to do something light, pure entertainment," Phoenix explained, and the part of the young Indiana in the movie *Indiana Jones and the Last Crusade* was ideal.

The opening scene of this third Indy adventure fell to Phoenix. The 10-minute, all-action sequence was set in Utah in the year 1912 where, in true comic-book style, a group of swarthy men hovered over a treasure trove with greedy grins on their bearded faces, watched from behind a rock by two teenage boys. One of these is the young Indiana who, discovered by the bad guys, heads off on a chase sequence which takes him from horseback to the top of a circus train full of animals, to a pit of snakes, to an encounter with a rhino and a lion—whence Indy obtains his trademark whip and scar on the chin. Typically, Phoenix opted to do the stunts himself. "It would have been lying," he said, "to have someone else to do the stunts."

Indiana Jones and the Last Crusade was one of the biggest hits of 1989, second in box-office takings only to Tim Burton's *Batman*. Now more than ever, River Phoenix was the name on the lips of Hollywood's agents, but even so, Phoenix turned down the lead role in George Lucas's spin-off TV series *The Young Indiana Jones Chronicles*.

River received the 1991 Venice Film Festival Best Actor Award for his role in My Own Private Idaho

LETTING GO

It was at this point that Arlyn Phoenix saw the opportunity to enact the next stage of her plan for her family—a move away from the perils of California. Hollywood may have been providing the Phoenix family unit with a handsome income, but Arlyn saw no reason to succumb to the lifestyle. "We didn't get caught up in the parties or the lifestyle," she informed the magazines. "We saw what was happening and we said, 'There's no way to raise kids there.'" The kids had to stay, however, until a move was financially viable: "We couldn't do it until we knew that we could go away and he would still be offered parts."

The Phoenix family bought land near Gainesville, Florida, an area with about 90,000 people. They settled on a 20-acre site in the small town of Micanopy, population 600, eight miles south of the university city. "Camp Phoenix" was custom-built at the end of a dirt track leading from Route 441. A stream ran through the property and the house had three large bedrooms—one for the boys, River and Leaf; one for the girls, Rain, Summer, and Liberty; and one for the parents and office use. It was reputedly filled with tapestries, Greenpeace posters, and Gaia books. John Phoenix handed over the management of his son's career to Arlyn and planted an organic garden for their food.

River soon moved to a rented house of his own—but only as far away as Gainesville. The small town found him polite

With his band, Aleka's Attic

and unassuming—he even appeared at local school work-shops on the environment. But there were some far-reaching changes going on in the young star's life. His relationship with Martha Plimpton was already under strain. She was landing parts in a succession of films, and they could rarely meet. (A friend of Plimpton's claimed that the actress broke off the relationship after the 1989 Oscar ceremony because she realized Phoenix was beginning to dabble in drugs.) Meanwhile, River and Rainbow returned to their mutual childhood love of music and together started a band called Aleka's Attic, in which River played guitar and wrote songs and Rainbow sang. They rehearsed up at their parents' place, played benefits at events like Rock Against Fur and performed at a fashionable low-rent sort of place called Hardback Café. There River met Suzanne Solgot, a massage therapist four years his senior, who played in an all-girl punk band and moved in to share his house.

Aleka's Attic released only one recording—a song on *Tame Yourself*, a fund-raising compilation for PETA (People for the Ethical Treatment of Animals). k.d. lang and the B-52's contributed to the same album, as did REM, whose singer, Michael Stipe, became a close friend. Phoenix was soon said to "idolize" Michael Balzary, a.k.a. Flea, bassist from the Red Hot Chili Peppers, and John Frusciante, once of the same band, became another close friend. If, as many were to claim, it was the music scene that fatally introduced River Phoenix to drugs, it was now that his fate was being sealed.

For the next couple of films, Phoenix was only coasting, feeling for a direction in fully adult roles with a comedy ensemble role in Lawrence Kasdan's *I Love You to Death* (1990) and the lead in Nancy Savoca's offbeat *Dogfight* (1991). *I Love You to Death* saw River as Devo Nod, pizza cook, mystic, follower of Eastern religion, and earnest admirer of Rosalie (Tracey Ullman), wronged wife of philan-dering pizzeria owner Joey Boca (Kevin Kline). When harm-less young Devo is drawn by his love of Rosalie to make a fumbling intervention in her attempt to murder her husband, he succeeds only in bringing the two closer together. The film was notable for teaming Phoenix with Keanu Reeves (who has a cameo as a bungling spaced-out would-be killer) on screen for the first time — and for the fact that, to get into character, River learned to make pizza.

River's gauche Devo didn't have a love scene and never got closer to his idolized Rosalie than reading her runes. A further shock to the fan club came with Phoenix's first leading-man role as a marine in Nancy Savoca's *Dogfight*. This was the first film where the casting of Phoenix gave the green light to the movie. (The studio was nonetheless worried that Phoenix's buzz-cut hairstyle would put off his female following and insisted on blond highlights in his hair.)

Set in San Francisco in 1963, the film features Phoenix as Edward Baines Birdlace, a young marine who has been given a final night's shore liberty with his friends before shipping out to Vietnam. They decide to hold a "dog fight," a cruel contest in which the group pool their money, rent a bar, and see who can find the ugliest date. The marine with the best "dog" wins the cash. Phoenix's character finds himself falling for his date, Rose (Lili Taylor), a plump would-be singer who writes poetry and listens to Joan Baez.

Once again, Phoenix went to great lengths to get into the part. Director Savoca arranged an abbreviated boot-camp experience for Phoenix and the other actors playing marines, and two former drill instructors put them through their paces for four days. According to costar Anthony Clark, River got a little more into character than was necessary: "On the first night we're out of boot camp we went to this party, and it ended up that the police were called. River was the head of that whole thing. He had a mean streak. He wanted to get into a fight. That night he was a marine."

But if River was beginning to push himself to new horizons for his parts, it was his next role that truly took him to the edge and from which, it would seem, he never recovered. *My*

They Died Too Young

Own Private Idaho, Gus Van Sant's tender, offbeat, independent movie, was the film that rocketed River Phoenix to cult stardom. His performance was to secure him his first comparisons with James Dean. Phoenix played Mike Water, a narcoleptic lonesome hustler searching for the lost warmth of his mother's love, the truth about his never-known father, and the love of his rich-boy-taken-to-the-streets friend Scott Favor, played by Keanu Reeves.

In parts mesmeric, in parts esoteric (Van Sant's script took the form of a road movie with elements borrowed from Shakespeare's *Henry IV, Part I,* its dialogue a blend of contemporary street slang and Shakespearean speech), *Idaho* cast its gently hypnotic spell far from the mainstream of movies. In one scene, a group of real-life hustlers exchange stories in a dingy coffee bar. In another set piece, the covers of gay porn magazines come to life with pop-art brio. Perhaps most memorably, Water's narcoleptic trances are accompanied by fleeting images of extraordinary beauty: leaping fish in a silver stream; a lonely road stretching to the horizon; a bank of quickly moving clouds; a house falling from the heavens.

Gus Van Sant wanted River Phoenix for Waters because he sensed a part of that character in the young actor. "*Idaho* is the story of a rich boy who falls off the hill and a kid on the street," Van Sant explained. "I saw a bit of the hill in Keanu's personality and a bit of the street in River's. They played out those extensions of themselves."

Phoenix, for his part, took Van Sant's trust to heart. He worked with real-life narcoleptic Jake, the inspiration for Mike Waters, until he had a complete understanding of the curious sleep fits. More dangerously, he researched life on the streets. Asked if he hung out with the kids in Portland, Oregon, his reply was, "Totally." Asked how he researched the lifestyle of street hustlers, he explained: "I entered it through friends of Gus's who were already on the street, Scott and Gary. Some street kids came over to Gus's house, and we met different people at different places. But the actual street stuff was just us working on our own time. Like guerrillas. Gus's choice was to use real street guys or us, so Keanu and I felt a great burden." Far from being disappointed, Van Sant feared Phoenix's immersion into his role was so extreme that the actor was changing into his character.

This dedication won River the Best Actor Award at the Venice Film Festival that year, but *Idaho* was a risky project for someone of his star-status to take on and one that surely marked a diversion from the career path chosen for him by his parents. It was, at heart, a film about love. Phoenix was drawn to the subject ("I have really strong feelings about the search for home and mother. I though it was very, very touching") and contributed to the script of the campfire scene, making overt his character's hidden needs when he murmurs to Keanu Reeves, "I really want to kiss you, man." The Van Sant movie transformed him into a gay icon, but the fragility and vulnerability in his performance made audiences across the board feel protective toward him. In *Idaho* Phoenix's fragile beauty was at its most charismatic.

Idaho costar Keanu Reeves

Arriving for the 1989 Poitier Award ceremony

CLOSE TO THE EDGE

If Phoenix's seductive screen aura was to survive the movie's dangers unscathed, his personal life was to pay a greater price. The truth of what happened on *My Own Private Idaho* is not known. Nobody from that film (including director Gus Van Sant) will talk. But everyone in the film business has now heard the rumors. These suggest that River's heroin use began then, and began as a professional experiment as much as a social one —to help generate his brilliant portrait of a narcoleptic, gay, drug-using prostitute. *My Own Private Idaho* was an intense, collective experience. It is possible that, with Phoenix's family financially secure and with siblings Rainbow and Leaf also acting at the time and contributing to the family coffer, River felt able to enjoy some kind of belated adolescent rebellion. Something certainly changed after *Idaho*.

Gus Van Sant's collaborative, experimental methods gave the young actor a glimpse beyond the mainstream to an experience he clearly preferred. Now he wanted to try a stint behind the camera and to choose projects where he was more than just a pretty face attached to star-status name. "I want to buy a 16-millimeter camera," he declared. "I'm not committed to the idea of being a filmmaker, but I'd like to try some shorts. I really like documentaries." And aware of his lack of power in the movie machine, he made a "deal with the devil": one corporate film a year in return for the freedom to make two independent films. In what were to be the last two years of his too-short life, this led to a selection of movie roles from the banal to the bizarre.

The next movie could only have added to River's feeling of disillusionment and powerlessness. It was a far cry from *Idaho*. No doubt he had to take it to preserve his nice-kid image after his dive into the gutter. *Sneakers* (1992), directed by Phil Alden Robinson, writer-director of *Field of Dreams*, was a high-tech comedy caper about an offbeat computer-hacking security team that takes on an assignment to steal a "black box" containing security secrets. Phoenix played 19-year-old Carl Arbogast, the "kid" in an all-star team which had Robert Redford as its leader and Dan Aykroyd, Sidney Poitier, Ben Kingsley, and Mary McDonnell as its members. River was billed above Sidney Poitier, and his coming on board was a central factor in Universal giving a green light to the movie, but apart from a couple of cute moments and an amusing comedy disco-dance routine, he barely figures in what was a forgettable, unexceptional film. Phoenix was not proud of this performance. "I trashed myself in this," he said. "I've really degraded myself. He's very hyper, always twitching, the kind of guy you avoid playing if you want to walk with grace and dignity at the premiere."

Unverified tales of drugged, difficult behavior came in 1993 from the set of Phoenix's next film, Peter Bogdanovich's *The Thing Called Love*, and a glance at River Phoenix's troubled, gaunt appearance as guitar-wielding cowboy James Wright suggests they were true. Gone is the keen innocence of Phoenix's earlier roles. In its place is a misjudged, overbearing performance.

The film told the tale of four young country-western musicians trying to make a breakthrough in Nashville. Phoenix's James Wright is battling with Kyle (Dermot Mulroney, who was also to costar in Phoenix's next project,

They Died Too Young

Silent Tongue) for the heart of Miranda (Samantha Mathis). Phoenix was showcased live singing and playing guitar, and he wrote a song for the movie, "Lone Star State of Mind." But even though it was his name on the cast list that persuaded Paramount to give the project the go-ahead, Phoenix's performance struck a discordant note.

There was plenty going on offscreen. "He was crazy about Samantha right away," said Peter Bogdanovich. Samantha Mathis was to be the woman with whom River was to have his last relationship. Despite his new-found love, however, his drug abuse on location in Tennessee was so serious that one night's filming featuring Phoenix was reportedly unusable.

An interview from the set, published posthumously in the British newspaper the *Mail on Sunday*, gives stark insight into River Phoenix's rapidly deteriorating state. Tom Daniels was shocked by Phoenix's unkempt appearance ("He looked like a 23-year-old who had been up all night") and by his rambling, shivering, and incoherence. His conversation was riddled with confusion and distress. "I'm being jerked around in the way you're always jerked around," he told Daniels. "They want you to do what they want you to do. I have 20 personalities on top of the 10 I already have. So now I have 30 people in my head." He made no attempt to disguise his unhappiness ("I sleep and I work and that's it. I don't do anything fun for myself. I have to immerse myself or I feel false") or his growing frustration: "Sometimes I do a take to pacify executives and it winds up in the movie and I'm kicking myself."

It was whispered knowledge on the set of *The Thing Called Love* that Phoenix was a mixed-up kid who had what was vaguely referred to as a drug problem. But friends say no one with any power in the industry inquired too deeply into just how mixed-up he was for fear of upsetting the money machine of his image as a sexy saint. At the end, friends say he just gave in to the drugs, trying to disguise the creeping clues to his abuse—the bloodshot eyes, the incoherence, the fragile frame—by working out at a gym with a personal trainer.

He became edgy and moody. At parties he would just play his own "original compositions" on the guitar. At a wedding at which even the Red Hot Chili Peppers conformed and wore tuxedos, Phoenix turned up in sneakers, ripped shorts, and a dirty T-shirt. A British actor living in Hollywood testified to Phoenix's heavy use of cocaine. The actor would call Phoenix at the St. James's Club, a grand white 1930s apartment block-turned-hotel which River frequented, and they would meet to drink vodka and snort and free-base cocaine. The British actor, "Charles" was also testing the liquid designer-drug GHB (Gamma Hydroxybutric acid). Much discussed in reports of River's death, GHB had previously made headlines when it caused rocker Billy Idol to collapse in convulsions. "Charles" never saw Phoenix use it, but Taki, a columnist in the English magazine the *Spectator,* quoted an actress friend's account of a visit from Phoenix which included his use of GHB, as well as cocaine and morphine.

River lets off steam onstage

As a pizza chef in I Love You to Death

TOO MUCH TOO YOUNG

It must have been the increasingly dark side of Phoenix's nature that chose his last complete role as Talbot Roe in Sam Shepard's Wild West ghost story, *Silent Tongue* (1993). When Talbot Roe's half-Indian wife Awbonnie dies in childbirth, he becomes crazed with grief and sits in lonely vigil in the middle of a desolate prairie guarding her body in a burial tree. Most of River's time on screen is spent rolling his eyes and howling. A suitably macabre final bow.

For the six weeks before his death, River had been out on location in the desert, 300 miles south of Salt Lake City, near a little town called Torrey. He was filming *Dark Blood,* another of his esoteric movie choices, full of caves, candles, and soliloquies against the sky, which had Jonathan Pryce and Judy Davis as city types in an encounter with Phoenix's alternately charming and terrifying character called only Boy.

Directed by Dutch art-house director George Sluzier, whose 1988 chiller *Spoorloos* (*The Vanishing*) brought him a crossover into Hollywood, the production was not a happy one. Jonathan Pryce recalled premonitions of disaster during the filming. "River said, 'Somebody is going to die on this film.' We were on this kind of inexorable journey to disaster. Every day there was some kind of difficulty. It just seemed as if something had to give." River phoned William

Richert from the set and left a message on his answering machine: "I'm out here in Utah, and I'm having a hard time keeping my head above water in this crazy business."

The location work over, River went back to Los Angeles to start on scenes set inside the hut where Boy lived. He was put up in the Nikko Hotel on La Cienga Boulevard—a big Japanese business hotel with a waterfall and great quantities of marble in its lobby. He worked on Saturday, but he had Sunday off, so he was going to have fun. (He was never to return, the half-complete movie had to be scrapped, and in two separate lawsuits, his estate was to be sued after his death to the tune of $5.5 million for breach of contract due to the use of illegal drugs.)

Hotel witnesses confirm that Phoenix and his friends had started partying early that Sunday. Room service delivered drinks and food and noted the chaos, the loud music, and the spaced-out look on Phoenix's face. They knew it was a drug high, but they still brought the drinks. At 10:30 P.M. Phoenix asked that his car be brought around. He and his friends made a rowdy exit from the hotel lobby. Someone else drove, while River slumped in the back.

They were on their way to the Viper, where River and his friends, some of whom were part of Aleka's Attic, were intending to jam with other musicians. At the club, River was joined by his brother Leaf, his sister Rain, and his girlfriend, Samantha Mathis. They sat at a table off the dance floor and ordered drinks. A waitress noted that River was stoned on arrival: "He was barely able to stand, and he kept leaping up and bumping into things. His words were so blurred you could hardly understand him."

Eyewitness reports give conflicting evidence of the final hours of River's short life. Some claim Phoenix went to a small room behind the stage with a friend and shot up a speedball —the same kind of lethal combination of heroin and cocaine that had killed John Belushi 11 years before. Others say River stayed seated and threw back glass after glass of highly potent

German Jägermeister. Another story had him dancing around the room in a frenzy of activity, while a rare on-the-record account from club regular Heather McDougal claims there was nothing at all unusual about Phoenix's behavior that night.

But everyone at the Viper on that fateful night agrees on the sequence of events that filled River's last minutes at the club. Sitting at the table, Phoenix became terribly ill and began to vomit on himself. His friends took him to the washroom to clean him up. They splashed cold water on his face and tried to stop him trembling; then they got him back to the table. By now he was showing serious signs of overdose. He began having seizures, and then he slumped and slid under the table. Fighting for breath, he asked to be taken outside for fresh air. Leaf, Rain, and Samantha Mathis helped him outside (some say that on his way out he called out, "I'm going to die, dude"), and there on the pavement in the dark hours of Halloween the fragile young star who still had so much promise played out his death in the full glare of publicity.

The circumstances puzzled police and were investigated by homicide detectives. "There's no way of knowing what precipitated his death," said Bill Martin, a spokesman for the Los Angeles County Sheriff's Department. The police were called in "because it is unusual for someone of this age to die like this." But the investigation ruled out any foul play. A coroner's report found no signs of needle marks on River's body and concluded that the drugs had been either "inhaled or ingested."

How did it happen? River Phoenix had been known as one of the most clean-living stars in Hollywood. He was famous for being a strict teetotaler and vegetarian who used nothing that originated from animals—including eggs, cheese, and honey. His mother, Arlyn, would whip up tofu scrambles for him on the set. His only vice was thought to be his smoking of chemical-free organic tobacco. The family thrived on vegetarianism and the avoidance of modern medicine. "I've refused to have them inoculated," Arlyn said. "I've never given them an aspirin. If some awful illness happened in our family . . . then I'd look at it as a challenge to heal ourselves with herbs and spiritual enlightenment." River was the child of people with an uncompromising ideology of alternative living.

In his later years, though, he struck out on a different, more dangerous path. Everyone was apt to pass the buck for what happened. The film industry blames Phoenix's musical connection—everyone knows, they say, that in L.A.'s music clubs, favorite hangouts for the young, hip, and cool, drugs circulate frequently among the clientele. Still others point a finger at River's "pushy" mother Arlyn, who now prefers to be known as "Heart," for bequeathing her eldest son an impossible burden.

Certainly the breach between River Phoenix's uneducated faith and the Hollywood machine which grasped his ideals and spat them out as so many press releases proved too great. As a chasm opened between his private and public life, River lost his footing. "I am confused," he told his ever-hungry interviewers. "I go back and forth about success and wealth and want to take the Devil's bribe and use it for God."

He still spoke of founding a home for abused kids, the homeless, the mentally ill, of opening a theater in a small town, of setting up a touring educational seminar group. He succeeded in buying 800 acres of forest on the border of Panama and Costa Rica.

But he had to push his true self further and further from sight. "Depending on the interviewer and the publication, I lie all the time," he told Britain's *Time Out*. "They'll change the truth anyhow so I may as well say what I like. I am a kind of minute commodity, my name is no longer my own." He thought his only refuge was to immerse himself in the make-believe of his roles—or drugs.

There was a small, private memorial service for River Phoenix in Hollywood. Among the close friends who spoke

They Died Too Young

at his memorial were directors Peter Bogdanovich and Rob Reiner, actresses Helen Mirren and Christine Lahti, *Running on Empty* writer Naomi Foner, River's agent, Iris Burton, his sisters, Rain, Liberty, and Summer. River's mother spoke the final tribute. Flea from the Red Hot Chili Peppers, REM singer Michael Stipe, and actor Dan Aykroyd also attended. There was singing and dancing. Leaf, who was with him when he died, and his father, John, chose to remain at home in Florida with his ashes. River had been cremated the week before.

River's death not only left behind the films he did, but the knowledge of what might have been. There were parts lined up into the future, many of them continuing Phoenix's descent into the darker side of life. He was due to start shooting the pivotal role of the interviewer, Daniel, in the Tom Cruise vehicle *Interview with the Vampire* on November 30 (the recasting of this role brought another posthumous lawsuit to the tune of $500,000); John Boorman was going to feature him alongside Sean Connery and Winona Ryder in *Broken Dreams;* there was to be a part in the film of Dennis Cooper's grotesque tale *Frisk*; Gus Van Sant, whose recent *Even Cowgirls Get the Blues* had featured Rain Phoenix, was likely to cast him as the young Andy Warhol. And what no doubt seemed most important to River himself was that at the time of his death, he had 15 songs on a demo tape and was close to signing a record contract.

But all this would only exist in the imaginations of his bereft fans. A small, dedicated group kept vigil outside the Viper Room, bringing flowers and burning candles to a pavement shrine. "A true individual who will be remembered," said one note; "The Eternal River Flows" read an inscription on a watercolor.

The man-child of great beauty and seriousness was gone, but not forgotten.

CHRONOLOGY

1970 River Jude born to parents Arlyn and John on a commune in Madras, Oregon, on August 23. (Original family name unknown.)

1977 Family takes the last name "Phoenix" to celebrate their return to the United States after spending several years in Central and South America as missionaries.

1979-1980 Wins many prizes in local talent contests; the family moves to Hollywood where River begins doing TV commercials; performs audience warm-ups for the TV variety show *Real Kids*.

1982 Plays youngest brother Guthrie McFadden in the CBS drama *Seven Brides for Seven Brothers*.

1984 Works on the NBC miniseries *Celebrity; Backwards: The Riddle of Dyslexia* (after-school special); *It's Your Move* (NBC pilot).

1985 Plays Robert Kennedy Jr. in *Robert Kennedy and His Times*; guest stars on *Family Ties;* makes his big screen debut in the science fiction adventure *Explorers*.

1986 Plays Chris Chambers in the Rob Reiner film *Stand By Me*, Charlie Fox in *The Mosquito Coast* co-starring Harrison Ford, and Chris Benfield in the television movie *Circle of Violence: A Family Drama*.

1987 *A Night in the Life of Jimmy Reardon* and *Little Nikita* open.

1989 Nominated for Academy Award for Best Supporting Actor for his performance in *Running on Empty*; plays the young Indiana Jones in *Indiana Jones and the Last Crusade*. Forms the band Aleka's Attic with his sister Rainbow.

1990 Feature film *I Love You to Death* released.

1991 Stars in *Dogfight*; wins a Venice Film Festival Award for Best Actor for his performance in *My Own Private Idaho*.

1992 Joins all-star cast of Robert Redford, Dan Aykroyd, Sidney Poitier, Ben Kingsley, and Mary McDonnell in the high-budget comedy *Sneakers;* used drugs throughout the filming of the 1993 movies *The Thing Called Love* and *Silent Tongue*.

1993 Collapses at the Viper Room in Los Angeles following massive overdoses of cocaine and heroin and dies on October 31.

The Red Hot Chili Peppers, friends of River Phoenix

INDEX